Robert Potter

An Inquiry Into Some Passages in Dr. Johnson's Lives of the Poets

Poets

Particularly his observations on lyric poetry, and the odes of Gray

Robert Potter

An Inquiry Into Some Passages in Dr. Johnson's Lives of the Poets
Particularly his observations on lyric poetry, and the odes of Gray

ISBN/EAN: 9783744774918

Printed in Europe, USA, Canada, Australia, Japan

Cover: Foto ©Thomas Meinert / pixelio.de

More available books at **www.hansebooks.com**

A N

INQUIRY

INTO SOME PASSAGES IN

Dr. *Johnson*'s Lives of the Poets:

PARTICULARLY.

HIS OBSERVATIONS ON

LYRIC POETRY,

AND

THE ODES OF GRAY.

———

BY R. POTTER.

———

LONDON:

PRINTED FOR J. DODSLEY, PALL-MALL.

———

M.DCC.LXXXIII.

AN

INQUIRY, &c.

JUST Criticifm, directed by fuperior learning and judgement, and tempered with candor, muft at all times have an happy influence on the public tafte, and of courfe be favourable to the interefts and credit of literature. It is well known how much the age, in which he lived, was enlightened and refined by Mr. Addifon; his judgement was juft, his manner fimple and elegant, and from his tafte there is no appeal; his page was, like the vernal fun, bright and gentle; it gradually and imperceptibly difpelled the mifts of barbarifm which hung over learning, and fpread an intellectual light, the influence of which was univerfal and permanent. Every age is not fo happy as to produce an Addifon; yet the prefent age owes much to the vigorous and manly underftanding of Dr. Johnfon: this truly refpectable writer was early and defervedly diftinguifhed by his great abilities, and the public

B   has

has fo long been habituated to receive and fubmit to his de-
cifions, that they are now by many confidered as infallible.
Some years ago he wrote the life of Savage, a man neither
amiable nor virtuous, but of a fingular character formed from
fingular circumftances of diftrefs, which never happened before, probably will never happen again in the life of any other
man : undeferved diftrefs has a claim to pity ; and pity has
always in it fome mixture of love, which wifhes to palliate the
failings of the unfortunate fufferer ; Dr. Johnfon has the
feelings of humanity warm at his honeft heart ; he has therefore
with a free and fpirited indignation ftigmatized the unnatural
mother, and to her unrelenting cruelty ultimately refers the
faults of the unhappy fon, faults which truth would not allow
him to fupprefs, nor his virtue incline him to defend.   In
his account of Savage as a Poet, he places his genius in the
faireft light, and makes juft apologies for his inaccuracies.
This little tract was written with an animated glow of fentiment, a vigorous and clear expreffion, and a pleafing candor
fometimes perhaps ftretched a little beyond the line of judgement : it pleafed ; it muft always pleafe : no wonder then
that the public expreffed no fmall degree of fatisfaction, when
it was known that this celebrated author was engaged in
writing the Lives of the moft eminent Englifh Poets, with
critical obfervations on their works ; much was expected from
his knowledge and judgement ; but high raifed expectations
are frequently difappointed : in thefe volumes, amidft the
many juft obfervations, the folid fenfe, and deep penetration
which even his enemies muft admire, his warmeft friends find
fome paffages which they muft wifh unwritten or obliterated.

It

It is not my intention to follow the Biographer through all the lives he has written; but, after a few cursory remarks, these pages will be confined to his observations on Lyric Poetry, particularly on the Odes of Mr. Gray. As I shall have frequent occasions to dissent from the Critic's judgement, I shall give my reasons freely and firmly, but with great respect to his understanding and virtues.

" With the political tenets of the writer, I have nothing to do; my business is with his criticism:" yet it were to be wished that the spirit of party had not been so warmly diffused through this work; it is often disagreeable, but in the Life of Milton it is disgusting: not that I am inclined to defend the religious or political principles of our great poet; I know too well the intolerant spirit of that liberty, which worked its odious purposes through injustice, oppression, and cruelty; but it is of little consequence to the present and future ages whether the author of Paradise Lost was Papist or Presbyterian, Royalist or Republican; it is the Poet that claims our attention : if however in the life of Milton it were necessary to take notice of the part he bore in those disastrous times, it might have been more eligible to have imitated the moderation of J. Philips, who, though he wrote more than seventy years nearer those times, when the facts were yet fresh on mens memories, checked his expression of the abhorrence of them, through respect to his master, with this beautiful apostrophe,

> And had that other Bard,
> Oh, had but he, that first ennobled song

With

With holy raptures, like his Abdiel been,
'Mongſt many faithleſs, ſtrictly faithful found;
Unpity'd he ſhould not have wail'd his orbs,
That roll'd in vain to find the piercing ray,
And found no dawn, by dim ſuffuſion veil'd!
But he——However, let the Muſe abſtain,
Nor blaſt his fame, from whom ſhe learn'd to ſing
In much inferior ſtrains.——

We are alſo ſorry to ſee the maſculine ſpirit of Dr. Johnſon deſcending to what he perhaps in another might call "anile garrulity." In reading the life of any eminent perſon we wiſh to be informed of the qualities which gave him the ſuperiority over other men: when we are poorly put off with paltry circumſtances, which are common to him with common men, we receive neither inſtruction nor pleaſure. We know that the greateſt men are ſubject to the infirmities of human nature equally with the meaneſt; why then are theſe infirmities recorded? Can it be of any importance to us to be told how many pair of ſtockings the author of the Eſſay on Man wore? Achilles and Therſites eat, and drank, and ſlept; in theſe things the Hero was not diſtinguiſhed from the Buffoon: are we made the wiſer or the better by being informed that the Tranſlator of Homer ſtewed his Lampreys in a ſilver ſaucepan? Who does not bluſh when he finds recorded that idle ſtory of a nameleſs critic, who ſaid of the author of the Fleece, *He will be buried in woolen?* Is this held up for wit? Is it intended as a ſarcaſm on Dyer? Is it not an inſult to the underſtanding of the reader? Let me ſtop a moment to ſpeak

of

of this writer. " Dyer is not a poet of bulk or dignity fufficient to require an elaborate criticifm." Does Dr. Johnfon
eftimate poetical merit, as Rubens did feminine beauty, *by the
ftone?* Well then might he recommend Blackmore to us. If
the Fleece be now univerfally neglected, let me join my teftimony to that of Akinfide, that fuch neglect is a reproach to
the reigning tafte; the poem is truly claffical : to fay that
" Dyer's mind was not unpoetical," is parfimonious praife; he
had a benevolent heart, a vigorous imagination, and a chaftifed
judgement; his ftyle is compact and nervous; his numbers
have harmony, fpirit, and force,

> On they move
> Indiffolubly firm ; nor obvious hill,
> Nor ftreit'ning vale, nor wood, nor ftream divides
> Their perfect ranks.——

The prefent paffion for anecdotes may make thefe levities
pardonable : but when the narrative goes further, and reflects
upon the focial and moral character of a worthy perfon, it
muft be taken up in an higher tone. We are carefully informed of the avidity of Addifon, of the eagernefs with which
he laid hold on his proportion of the profits arifing from the
papers of the Spectator, of his unmerciful exaction of an
hundred pounds lent by him to Steele. If this be true, it
only fhows that Addifon had not " exalted his moral to di-
vine :" but the intervention of more than fixty years has not
yet obliterated the remembrance of his gentle manners and benevolent difpofition : that Steele was not an œconomift is well
known ; but what authority Dr. Johnfon has for faying that

Addifon

Addifon reclaimed his loan by an execution, we are not told: I am told by the beft authority that it is an abfolute falfe-hood. This vindication is due to the memory of a man, who was univerfally refpected whilft he lived, and " of whofe virtue it is a fufficient teftimony, that the refentment of party has tranfmitted no charge of any crime;" "who taught, with great juftnefs of argument and dignity of language, the moft important duties, and fublime truths;" " who employed wit on the fide of virtue and religion, purified intellectual plea-fure, feparated mirth from indecency," enlightened and re-fined the age in which he lived, " and excited fuch an emula-tion of intellectual elegance, that, from his time to our own, life has been gradually exalted, and converfation purified and enlarged."

This purity, this enlargement leads us to refent the cruel manner in which Dr. Johnfon fpeaks of the Lady, who is the fubject of Hammond's Elegies: an old Goth would not have been guilty of fuch an indelicacy: but whatever character her lover, or his Biographer, may have bequeathed her, thofe, who were fo happy as to be acquainted with her, fpeak of her as a very excellent and amiable woman. This offence againft truth and good manners is the more inexcufable, as Dr. John-fon had opportunities enough of informing himfelf of the Lady's real character. With regard to Hammond, whether Mr. Shiels was mifled by falfe accounts I cannot determine; but that this Poet was not the Son of Anthony Hammond, who was allied to Sir Robert Walpole by marrying his Sifter, I can affure the public upon the authority of that refpectable family. His Elegies certainly have faults, which the Critic

is

is eagle-eyed to difcover; but they have beauties, againft
which he fhuts his eyes; a younger man might perhaps fay
with Spenfer,

> Such one's ill judge of love, that cannot love,
> Ne in their frozen hearts feel kindly flame.
> For-thy they ought not thing unknown reprove,
> Ne natural affection faultlefs blame.

" Why Hammond, *or other writers*, have thought the qua-
train of ten fyllables elegiac, it is difficult to tell." Perhaps the difficulty is not great; the next fentence may ferve
to explain it; " the character of the Elegy is gentlenefs and
tenuity;" no other meafure in the Englifh language glides
with fuch eafy fweetnefs, and in fuch a gentle ftrain of melody.
" But this Stanza has been pronounced by Dryden, whofe
knowledge of Englifh metre was not inconfiderable, to be
the moft magnificent of all the meafures which our language
affords." The critic himfelf accounts for this opinion of Dryden, " Davenant was perhaps *at this time* his favourite author,
though Gondibert never appears to have been popular; and
from Davenant he learned to pleafe his ear with the ftanza of
four lines alternately rhymed." The elegant Aikins, in their
differtation on Gondibert, have adverted to its meafure with
propriety and fine tafte. But it is not for nothing that this opinion of Dryden is held out to us: Mr. Gray's Elegy is written
in this metre; it had been too defperate to have hazarded an
open attack on that poem; the Critic therefore fhelters himfelf
behind the authority of Dryden, and feems to direct his cenfure
againft Hammond, whilft the fhaft is aimed at Gray.

It

It is pleafant enough to find this writer, who has fo long dictated to the public tafte, and that in a pretty high tone, gravely doubting whether the art of Gardening, in the prefent enlarged acceptation of the word, demands any great powers of mind: the manner, in which he puts the queftion, plainly fhows his own opinion; but whatever " a fullen and furly fpeculator may think," the true judge of beautiful nature will efteem it an elegant exertion of real genius. But the tafte-lefs ridicule on Shenftone is only the introduction to a cruel and unjuft reflection on Lord Lyttelton. " For awhile the in-habitants of Hagley affected to tell their acquaintance of the little fellow that was trying to make himfelf admired; but when by degrees the Leafowes forced themfelves into notice, they took care to defeat the curiofity which they could not fupprefs, by conducting their vifitants perverfely to inconve-nient points of view, and introducing them at the wrong end of a walk to detect a deception; injuries of which Shenftone would heavily complain. Where there is emulation there will be vanity, and where there is vanity there will be folly." I refpect my reader, and my felf, too much to treat this malig-nant afperfion with the afperity it deferves. If the eminent virtues, the liberal difpofition, and benevolent heart of Lord Lyttelton could not fecure his character from fuch a rude at-tack, who may hope to efcape ? But happily the ftory carries its own confutation in itfelf: " the fpacious and opulent em-pire" can have no emulation of " the petty ftate, on which it looks with difdain." Can the majeftic Skiddow be a jealous rival of the little unanimated hills of Dovedale ? A candid writer will not record every idle tale he hears, which reflects

difhonour

dishonour on a great and good character; but when he is affured that the tale is falfe, it becomes his duty, as an honeft man, to retract it; Dr. Johnfon had this affurance from the moft honourable authority, which he ought to have refpected, and to have done juftice to the worthy inhabitants of Hagley. Detraction is an unamiable quality; " a man, faid an excellent perfon on this occafion, who could take a pleafure in defacing fine pictures, or mutilating exquifite ftatues, would be juftly odious; becaufe he would deprive elegant fpectators of the pleafure arifing from beautiful objects, and artifts of proper fubjects of imitation; but the man, who endeavours to deface and mutilate examples of virtue, is guilty of a much greater crime."

It is not without fome degree of honeft indignation that a perfon of candor obferves this fpirit of detraction diffufed fo univerfally through thefe volumes: of more than fifty of our Poets, whofe lives are here given, how few have paffed free from very fevere cenfures? the writer may have " been led to this beyond his intention;" but could it be " by the honeft defire of giving ufeful pleafure?" If the Man has the good fortune to efcape, the Poet is almoft fure to be condemned: the work puts one in mind of the wicker Coloffus of the Druids, in whofe chambers of tribulation an hecatomb of wretches was at once offered as victims to fome grim idol fuppofed to be propitiated by fuch horrid facrifices.

Many of thefe writers,

Like twinkling ftars the mifcellanies o'er,

C

were

were indeed but faint luminaries in the hemisphere of poetry; yet each shone with his portion of light, however small; and it was the Critic's province to discriminate their lustre, and to show how much, or how little, each contributed to the general brightness. To have considered how learning and taste were gradually improved by them, how our language was enriched, and the harmony of its numbers refined; to have ascertained with some degree of precision the various powers, the peculiar vein, the naïveté of each poet, would have been a curious and an useful investigation: this is done with much learning, judgement, and accuracy in the Life of Cowley; which gave the reader a reasonable expectation of continued entertainment and instruction; but he was soon disappointed; one indiscriminating censure hides the face of things, and we are left to wander undirected in this gloom,

> Quale per incertam lunam sub luce malignâ
> Est iter in sylvis, ubi cœlum condidit umbrâ
> Jupiter, et rebus nox abstulit atra colorem.

As the Poems of Pomfret, Yalden, and Watts, and the Creation of Blackmore were inserted in this collection by the recommendation of the Biographer, we may from thence form some judgement of his taste. He, who does not dislike Pomfret, may approve Yalden; he, who finds pleasure in Blackmore, may be enraptured with Watts. But this sagacious and penetrating Critic has the peculiar felicity of discovering that Blackmore " finds the art of uniting ornament with strength, and ease with closeness. This, he tells us is a skill which Pope

might

might have condefcended to learn from him, when he needed it fo much in his Moral Effays *". Of Blackmore's fkill, " his ratiocination and defcription," thefe lines from the Song of Mopas, annexed to his Life, are an happy fpecimen ;

> He fpread the pure cerulean fields on high,
> And arch'd the chambers of the vaulted fky,
> Which he, to fuit their glory with their height,
> Adorn'd with globes, *which reel as drunk with light.*

Further inftances of this Critic's want of tafte I leave to the obfervation of others ; he may foon hear of them from a very ingenious and refpectable writer, who wants not fpirit or ability to do juftice to the injured Poets : my bufinefs is to attend him into the regions of Lyric Poetry. His good fenfe led him to reprobate that lax and lawlefs verfification, which, under the name of Pindaric Odes, had long been a difgrace to Poetry and Pindar ; but it is with fome degree of aftonifhment that we find him fo warm in his commendations of Dryden's Poem on the death of Mrs. Killigrew ; this, he fays, " is undoubtedly the nobleft Ode that our language ever produced. The firft part flows with a torrent of enthufiafm. Fervet, immen-

---

* The revival of thefe Poems, the commendation of Blackmore, and the cenfure of Pope, gave occafion to the following Epigram.

Similes habent labra lectucas.

> Yon Afs in vain the flow'ry lawns invite ;
> To mumble thiftles his fupreme delight.
> Such is the Critic, who with wayward pride
> To Blackmore gives the praife to Pope denied ;
> Wakes Yalden's embers, joys in Pomfret's lay,
> But fickens at the heav'n-ftrung lyre of Gray.

fufque

fufque ruit." This praife is finely expreffed, but unhappily it is not juft: what he fays of the Threnodia may be applied to this poem alfo; " its firft and obvious defect is the irregularity of its metre, to which the ears of that age, however, were accuftomed. What is worfe, it has neither tendernefs nor dignity, it is neither magnificent nor pathetick. He feems to look round him for images, which he cannot find, and what he has he diftorts by endeavouring to enlarge them." This is fevere, but juft criticifm. It would be trifling and invidious to call the attention of the reader to the feeble efforts of Yalden's lyre; yet this Critic fays that his Hymn to Darknefs " is for the moft part imagined with great vigour, and expreffed with great propriety :—the tenth ftanza is inexpreffibly beautiful." I tranfcribe it for the fatisfaction of the reader;

Thou doft thy fmiles impartially beftow,
And know'ft no difference below,
All things appear the fame by thee,
Though Light diftinction makes, Thou giv'ft equality.

Thefe are the lyrical productions which Dr. Johnfon commends; but he feems to have contented himfelf with a very inaccurate and unclaffical idea of this compofition, which long ago he thus expreffed, " The imagination of the firft authors of lyrick poetry was vehement and rapid, and their knowledge various and extenfive. Living in an age when fcience had been but little cultivated, and when the minds of their auditors, not being accuftomed to accurate infpection, were eafily dazzled by glaring ideas, they applied themfelves to inftruct rather by fhort fentences and ftriking
thoughts,

thoughts, than by regular argumentation ; and finding attention more fuccefsfully excited by fudden fallies and unex-
pected exclamations, than by the more artful and placid
beauties of methodical deduction, they loofed their genius to
its own courfe, paffed from one fentiment to another without
expreffing the intermediate ideas, and roved at large over the
ideal world with fuch lightnefs and agility that their footfteps
are fcarcely to be traced. From this accidental peculiarity
of the antient writers the criticks deduce the rules of lyrick
Poetry, which they have fet free from all the laws by which
other compofitions are confined, and allow to neglect the
niceties of tranfition, to ftart into remote digreffions, and
to wander without reftraint from one fcene of imagery to
another."—Rambler, N° 158.

This furely is a very unfcholarlike account. The firft
Lyric Poets, whofe fine productions have efcaped the devaf-
tations of time, felt the poetic enthufiafm in an high degree ;
they wrote not in barbarous times, but in the moft enlightened age of Greece ; they did not attempt to dazzle by glaring
ideas and fudden fallies, but they knew that rapture, not
argumentation, was the conftituent part of that fpecies of
poetry which they cultivated. The Ode originally was a
facred compofition, and employed in celebrating the praifes of
the gods ; hence that religious air of folemn grandeur which
in a manner hallows the performance ; fometimes it was of
the prophetic caft, and of courfe affumed a myfterious and
aweful obfcurity ; in thefe the fublime genius of Æfchylus
is unrivaled. It then defcended to fing the actions of Demi-
gods

gods and Heroes : this was the province of Pindar, and his excellence in it is inimitable ;

Ἀναξιφόρμιγγες ὕμνοι,
Τίνα θεὸν, τιν' ἥρωα,
Τίνα δ' ἄνδρα κελαδήσομεν;

Hence it appears that this composition not only allowed, but even required sudden and bold transitions, and the highest flights of imagination to which even the Epic Muse dared not aspire : she prescribed laws to herself, which confined her to one great action; and she pursues her plan with grave dignity: but the Lyric is a Muse of fire that rises on the wings of Extasy, and follows her Hero or her God from one glorious action to another, from earth to heaven. Yet we are unjust to these great writers, if we suppose that they gave a loose to their genius, and roved at random over the ideal world; they had judgement as well as imagination; and though they disdained to be in subjection to rules which have no relation to their province, yet they have their specific laws which they never transgress. Sublimity is the essential and characteristic perfection of the Ode; where this can be attained by " the placid beauties of methodical deduction," that artful course is pursued; but it is more often seized by a rapid and impetuous transition; yet this is always under the controul of some nice connexion, is never vague and wanton, never loses sight of its important object. The Ode is daring, but not licentious; though it is great, it disclaims " the proud irregularity of greatness."

Collins

Collins was the firft of our poets that reached its excellence: his mind was impreffed with a tender melancholy, but without any mixture of that fullen gloom which deadens its powers; it led him to the fofteft fympathy, that moft refined feeling of the human heart; his faculties were vigorous, and his genius truly fublime; his ftyle is clofe and ftrong, and his numbers in general harmonious. He was well acquainted with Æfchylus and Euripides, and drew deep from their fountains: his thoughts had a romantic caft, and his imagination a certain wild grandeur, which fometimes perhaps approaches to the borders of extravagance; but this led him to defcriptions and allegories wonderfully poetical; fuch for inftance is the Antiftrophe in his Ode to Liberty, and the firft part of his Ode to Fear; Æfchylus himfelf has not a bolder conception, and the grandeur of thought is as greatly expreffed. Dr. Johnfon fpeaks of this fublime Poet with a tendernefs which reflects honour on himfelf; he allows him fometimes to have fublimity and fplendor, but in the coldnefs of criticifm expreffes fome difapprobation of his allegorical imagery, and is unjuft to his harmony.

The want of a good tafte in a profeffed Critic is a mental blindnefs which totally incapacitates him for the difcharge of the high office he has affumed; but the want of good manners is an offence againft thofe laws of decorum which, by guarding the charities of fociety, render our intercourfe with each other agreeable: yet there is in fome perfons a blunt and furly humour, which prides itfelf in defpifing thefe laws of civility; and often with an awkward affectation of pleafantry they play their rude gambols to make mirth, and

Wallowing

Wallowing unwieldy, enormous in their gait,
Tempest the ocean.

To whatever liberal motive this conduct may possibly be imputed, we are told by an excellent writer that " there is a certain expression of style and behaviour which verges towards barbarism; and that it is a degree of barbarism to ascribe noblenefs of mind to arrogance of phrase or insolence of manners." If there is a writer who, more than others, has a claim to be exempted from this pelting petulance, Mr. Gray has that claim: his own polished manners restrained him from ever giving offence to any good man, his warm and chearful benevolence endeared him to all his friends; though he lived long in a college, he lived not *sullenly* there, but in a liberal intercourse with the wifest and most virtuous men of his time; he was perhaps the most learned man of the age, but his mind never contracted the rust of pedantry; he had too good an understanding to neglect that urbanity which renders society pleafing; his conversation was instructing, elegant, and agreeable; superior knowlege, an exquisite taste in the fine arts, and above all purity of morals and an unaffected reverence for religion made this excellent person an ornament to society and an honour to human nature.

From this pleafing recollection of the merits of the man I now turn to his Lyric Poetry, in which he shines with superior lustre. His Ode on the Spring has an elegance of composition, an harmony of numbers, a richnefs of fancy, and a glow of colouring not to be found in any other writer; it is in the brightest manner of Pindar, and has reached perfection by

10

blending

blending with those vivid images the softest shades of melancholy morality; it resembles the beautiful and virtuous Andromache, in her interview with Hector, smiling through her tears. "This Ode, says the Critic, has something poetical both in the language and the thought; but the language is too luxuriant, and the thoughts have nothing new.—The morality is natural, but too stale; the conclusion is pretty." Had the language been less luxuriant, the Ode had been less beautiful, and less adapted to the smiling season. The Thoughts, considered separately, may not be new; but who has ever combined such an assemblage of poetical images, and cloathed them in such a splendid diction? Others may have contemplated the race of man and the insect youth as fluttering alike through life's little day; but who has represented the gaudy insect as retorting on the moralist in a vein of philosophy so peculiarly suitable to the sportive kind? The images of Nature have for ages worn the same form, and the sober eye of Contemplation may always have viewed them in the same light; but the poet's skill in selecting, disposing, and adorning them gives them all the grace of novelty. The Critic objects to one word in this Ode; "there has of late, says he, arisen a practice of giving to adjectives, derived from substantives, the termination of participles; but I was sorry to see, in the lines of a scholar like Gray, the *honied* spring." Our language derives much grace and strength from conversions of a like nature, and has long been in possession of this word, which it is likely to retain upon the authority of Shakespear and Milton, at least till its impropriety be better proved. It is observable that the Latin language has its *mellitus*, formed upon

D   the

the fame conftruction, and its pureft and moft correct writers fcrupled not to make ufe of it.

A diftant profpect of Eton College infpires the Poet with that enthufiafm, which marks the genius of Lyric Poetry; in a glow of rapture he addreffes the holy Henry's towers, and thofe that crown the ftately heights of Windfor, the hills, the groves, the fields over which he had fo often ftrayed: the gales, which breathe from them, footh his foul, and give him a momentary fenfation of joy and youth. In the fame glow of enthufiafm he afks Father Thames what youths are now bathing in his ftream, or fporting on his banks: this happy race he follows through their paths of pleafure with the moft enchanting ftrains of poetry; but at length looks beyond their prefent chearful and thoughtlefs day to the various afflictions which may embitter their future life; thefe he pathetically defcribes, and concludes with a moral reflection on the various fufferings of mankind, and the folly of inquiring into diftant ills, the knowlege of which would deftroy prefent happinefs. Yet Dr. Johnfon fays " the Profpect of Eton College fuggefts nothing to Gray, which every beholder does not equally think and feel." How great is that fagacity, which difcovers the thoughts and feelings of others before they are declared? But the Critic perhaps only means, as before, that the thoughts have nothing new: on this fubject a candid and judicious inquirer fays, " in any fuppofed combination of circumftances one train of thought is, generally, moft obvious, and occurs fooneft to the underftanding; and it being the office of poetry to prefent the moft *natural* appearances, one cannot be much furprized to find a coincidence of reflection."—On Poetical Imitation.

Imitation.—The affectation of new thoughts is too apt to divert the mind from the fimple and genuine appearances of things, and ufually produces quaint and far-fetched conceits; as the Painter, who difdains to copy Nature or to follow the great mafters of defign, aims at a manner of his own, and inftead of the umbrageous pine or the knotty hardihood of the giant oak, gives us ftrait and flender ftems, a poverty of foliage, and a colouring which Nature never knew Mr. Gray had too good an underftanding and too fine a tafte to be a Manierift. The Critic proceeds, " His fupplication to Father Thames to tell him who drives the hoop or toffes the ball, is ufelefs and puerile. Father Thames has no better means of knowing than himfelf." Criticifm of this nature breathes a frigid air, which chills all the faculties of genius. Thefe im- perfonations and addreffes to woods, mountains and ftreams,

> Omnia quæ Phœbo quondam meditante, beatus
> Audiit Eurotas, juffitque edifcere lauros,

give to poetry a peculiar animation, and conftitutes one of her greateft beauties ; every thing hears her voice. Of that tender apoftrophe of Æneas to the afhes of Troy,

> Iliaci cineres, et flamma extrema meorum,
> Teftor, in occafu veftro nec tela, nec ullos
> Vitaviffe vices Danaûm, &c.

fhall it be faid that they could bear no teftimony to his pious valour, and had no better means of knowing it than Dido herfelf? Shall we lop from Milton that fublime addrefs of Satan to the Sun as ufelefs and puerile, becaufe the Sun had

no

no means of hearing his call? Or rather fhall we not, without regard to the oppofition of this arbitrary Critic, leave the free people of Parnaffus their antient right of addreffing the kings of the floods, and other poetical fovereigns?—" His epithet *buxom* health, the Critic fays, is not elegant; he feems not to underftand the word." Milton thought the word at leaft not inelegant; he has ufed it twice, perhaps in different fenfes. I leave Dr. Johnfon to fettle its precife meaning with that refpectable dealer in words Dr. Adam Littleton. Of Mr. Gray's language I fhall have occafion to fpeak elfewhere.

The Hymn to Adverfity has in a fupreme degree every excellence which dignifies this fpecies of poetry. It opens, like the fineft Odes of the great mafters of antiquity, with an addrefs to the goddefs, and enumerates her aweful attributes in a ftrain truly fublime; it then reprefents Jupiter as fending his darling child, Virtue, to be trained by this rugged Nurfe, before whofe frown Folly's idle brood difperfe; but Wifdom, Melancholy, Charity, Juftice, and Pity attend her fteps: it concludes with a fupplication to the goddefs not to appear in her Gorgon terrors, nor furrounded with her vengeful band; but to wear her more benign form, and bring her milder train, whofe influence foftens, not wounds the heart. The folemnity of thefe fentiments is ennobled by a grandeur of imagery, and the dignity of expreffion receives new graces from the fober harmony of the lyre. " Of this Hymn, we are told, the hint was at firft taken from

O Diva, gratum quæ regis Antium ;

but

but Gray has excelled his original by the variety of his senti-
ments, and by their moral application." Mr. Gray has told
us that the hint was taken from Antiftrophe I. of the firft cho-
ral ode in the Agamemnon of Æfchylus ; and it is in the true
fpirit of that fublime author : the third ftanza indeed catches a
feature from the Ode to Fortune, but it is highly improved
and dignified. " Of this piece, at once poetical and rational, I
will not, fays the Critic, by flight objections violate the dignity." This is a gracious forbearance, confidering his alacrity
in cenfuring : but it muft be obferved that this penurious praife
is all that is afforded to three beautiful and fublime Odes : critical obfervations, which only aim to point out the defects,
but overlook the beauties of an author, may be deemed fafti-
dious, certainly they are not candid.

I have before faid that the Ode on the Spring is in the
brighteft manner of Pindar ; and that the Hymn to Adverfity
is in the true fpirit of Æfchylus : this may require an explana-
tion. The Odes of the latter writer are accompaniments to his
Tragic Mufe, and as they attend her through the aweful fcenes
of mifery, terror, vengeance, and blood, they take their colouring from thence ; they become religious inquiries into the dif-
penfations of the gods, or melancholy reflections on the infta-
bility of human greatnefs, or obfcure predictions or gloomy
prefages of the dreadful cataftrophe of the drama : the elevated
genius of the author has often given them a terrible fublimity.
The Englifh reader is now, or may be, well acquainted with
this great writer ; it is therefore unneceffary to extend this obfervation further. Pindar was employed in a more pleafing,
at leaft in a more chearful tafk ; his Mufe was courted to cele-

brate

brate the victors in the public games of Greece ; his Odes are
feftal fongs recounting glories, conquefts, and joy ; they take
their colouring from their fubject ; every thing in them is
fplendid, animated, and gay ; or if at any time he is led to
confider adverfe fortune, or the vanity of human life, the reflection is generally fhort, he foon returns to his ufual chear-
fulnefs, and every thing around, like the face of Nature after a
fhower, becomes more frefh, more bright, and more fmiling :
his genius at the fame time was impetuous and rapid, and
carried him to the nobleft heights of the fublime.   That the
Englifh reader may be enabled to form fome idea of this Poet's
manner, however imperfect, I have ventured to give a tranfla-
tion of one of his Odes ; thofe, who are acquainted with the
original, will be fenfible of the difficulty of the tafk.

Mr. Gray calls the Progrefs of Poetry a Pindaric Ode : how
happily he has imitated the fmiling beauty, as well as the great
manner of his mafter, may eafily be feen.   The firft Stanza
rolls along in the fervor of enthufiafm, various, fweet, and
magnificent as its fubject.   Dr. Johnfon fays " he is one of
thofe that are willing to be pleafed, and therefore would gladly
find the meaning of this firft Stanza."   Had the Critic been
pleafed to find the meaning of Horace, he could not have fail-
ed of finding the fame pleafure from this paffage, the high
metaphorical expreffions of which are drawn from thence ;

> Monte decurrens velut amnis, imbres
> Quem fuper notas aluere ripas,
> Fervet, immenfufque ruit profundo
> Pindarus ore ;

Laurea

Laureâ donandus Apollinari,
Seu per audaces nova dithyrambos
Verba devolvit, numerifque fertur
Lege folutis.

So Cowley ftyles it an unnavigable fong; and the Poet here tells us, that " the fubject and fimile, as ufual with Pindar, are united ;" a beautiful and fublime inftance of which we have in the opening of the fixth Olympic Ode, to which I refer the learned reader. So much for the Critic's charge of confufion, nonfenfe, and impertinence in this Stanza. In the fecond, the addrefs to the Enchanting Shell is truly Pindaric, and its power to controul the frantic Paffions is expreffed in the noble imagery of that fublime author : yet the Critic fays " the fecond Stanza, exhibiting Mars's car and Jove's eagle, is unworthy of further notice. Criticifm difdains to chafe a fchool-boy to his common places." Criticifm needs not be fo difdainful. When the antient Mythology is introduced into times, and manners, and fubjects, to which it has no relation, it is puerile and juftly reprehenfible; but there are occafions and circumftances which feem to require its ufe; and in thefe to deny it a place is unreafonable prejudice, particularly as it abounds with poetical images, of which we have two fine inftances in this Stanza. The allufions of this Ode are of claffical antiquity; the car of Mars and * the eagle of Jupiter
have

* Mr. Gray modeftly fays, " this is a weak imitation of fome incomparable lines in the firft Pythian of Pindar." This was not faid without reafon: the Eagle is there fixed upon the fceptre of Jupiter; the image fhould have been preferved.

With

have the ſtamp of the ſame times with the Æolian lyre and the ſprings of Helicon.

The third Stanza charms us with a delightful aſſemblage of gay ideas;

> Softly ſweet, in Lydian meaſures,
> Soon he ſooth'd the ſoul to pleaſures;

and ſhows that he is equally maſter of thoſe airs which " lap the land in extaſy," as of that dreadful harmony which ap-palls the ſoul; here, if ever, the Graces ſtrung the lyre; σὺν Ͼκθυζώνοισι Χαριτεσσι γεγωνεῖ. Even Dr. Johnſon acknowleges that this Stanza " has ſomething pleaſing." But it is not al-lowed to paſs uncenſured. " Idalia's *velvet-green* has ſome-thing of cant. An epithet or metaphor drawn from Nature ennobles Art; an epithet or metaphor drawn from Art degrades

> With ruffled plumes, and flagging wing,

does not well expreſs ὠκεῖαν πτέρυγ' ἀμφοτέρωθεν χάλαξαις.

> ὁ δὲ κνώσσων
> ὑγρὸν νῶτον ἀιωρεῖ, τεαῖς
> ῥιπαῖσι καλασχόμενος,

is an appropriated image, which ſhows that the poet looked at nature with a painter's eye; it is omitted in the imitation. But in juſtice to Mr. Gray it muſt be acknowleged that his two laſt lines,

> Quench'd in dark clouds of ſlumber lie
> The terror of his beak, and light'nings of his eye,

are at leaſt equal to the great original: the image of Mars is far ſuperior: the hills of Thrace judiciouſly fix the locality in learned alluſion to the Rhodo-peian Orpheus; the repreſentation of the god curbing the fury of his car, and dropping his lance, is Mr. Gray's own.

Nature."

Nature." What then becomes of the vitrea unda, of the pictæ volucres, of the gay enamel'd colours of bloſſoms and fruits, of the embroider'd vale, the fringed banks, and all thoſe beautiful images drawn from Art, with which the beſt writers antient and modern have embelliſhed Nature ? The Arts in their infancy were obliged to borrow many terms from their rich parent Nature ; but as they advanced to maturity, they amply repaid the loan ; from that time the metaphor and the metonymy have ranged at will from Nature to Art, and from Art to Nature ; and as it is the province of Art to adorn Nature, ſo the terms of Art have the ſame happy effect in enriching language. On this head Dr. Johnſon will perhaps pay ſome deference to the authority of the learned Critic, who, comparing the ſtyle of Dryden with that of Pope, ſays " Dryden's page is a natural field, riſing into inequalities, and diverſified by the varied exuberance of abundant vegetation ; Pope's is a *velvet lawn*, ſhaven by the ſcythe, and levelled by the roller."

The Critic proceeds. " Of the ſecond ternary of ſtanzas, the firſt endeavours to tell ſomething, and would have told it, had it not been croſſed by Hyperion." He ſeems not to underſtand the Poet, though the meaning of the paſſage is clearly explained in a note ſubjoined to it. From the pleaſing ideas and captivating melody of the foregoing Stanza the attention of the reader is called in a graver ſtrain to the ills which attend human life ; yet even theſe, the Poet tells us, are cheared by the Muſe, as the ſickly dews and ſpectres of the night are diſpelled by the riſing ſun : he therefore does tell us ſomething, and ſomething very much to the purpoſe ; this ſtanza expreſſes a

E   philoſophical

philofophical truth with poetic elegance, and the claffical image of Hyperion croffes nothing, but is croffed by the perverfe fpirit of fombrous Criticifm.

" The fecond Stanza, fays the Critic, defcribes well enough the univerfal prevalence of Poetry; but I am afraid that the conclufion will not rife from the premifes. The caverns of the North and the plains of Chili are not the refidences of *Glory* and *generous Shame*." This is not faid, nor even implied. The general pofition is " the extenfive influence of poetic genius over the remoteft and moft uncivilized nations." The fragments of the Northern Bards here referred to, and particularly the Poems of Offian, (which, whoever was their author, founded from the caverns of the North) not only cheared the fhivering native's dull abode, but breathe the high fpirit of Glory and Liberty. The Mufe too deigns to hear the favage youth on the plains of Chili raife his wild notes to War and Love, with both which Glory and Liberty are in clofe connexion; fo that the conclufion will arife from the premifes, " Liberty, and the virtues that naturally attend on it, purfue the track of Poetry."

And this is a fine introduction to the next Stanza, which tells us that in the evil hour of flavery the Mufes left their Greece for the Latian plains; and that difdaining to dwell there with tyrant power and coward vice they next fought the fea-encircled coaft of Albion. The fighs of Greece for the lofs of Liberty and the Mufes are expreffed in fuch a fober ftrain of mournful melody as foftens and fubdues the foul. Of this the Critic fays " the third ftanza founds big with *Delphi*, and *Egean*, and *Iliffus*, and *Meander*, and *hallow'd fountain*, and

folemn

solemn sound; but in all Gray's Odes there is a kind of cumbrous splendor which we wish away." In like manner Virgil sounds big with Groves, and Forests, and Naids, and Parnassus, and Aonia, and Aganippe;

> Quæ nemora, aut qui vos saltus habuere, puellæ
> Naiades, indigno cum Gallus amore periret?
> Nam neque Parnassi vobis juga, nam neque Pindi
> Ulla moram fecere, neque Aonia Aganippe.

Milton imitates this big language,

> Where were ye, Nymphs, when the remorseless deep
> Clos'd o'er the head of your lov'd Lycidas?
> For neither were ye playing on the steep,
> Where your old Bards, the famous Druids, lie,
> Nor on the shaggy top of Mona high,
> Nor yet where Deva spreads her wisard stream.

The Bard Mason too must be poetical, and classical, and talk big; witness his address to the Muses,

> Stay then awhile, O stay, ye fleeting fair;
> Revisit yet nor hallow'd Hippocrene,
> Nor Thespiæ's groves; till with harmonious teen
> Ye sooth his shade, and flowly-dittied air.
> Such tribute pour'd, again ye may repair
> To what lov'd haunt ye whilom did elect;
> Whether Lycæus, or that mountain fair,

Trim

Trim Mænalus, with piny verdure deckt.
But now it boots you not in thefe to ftray,
Or yet Cyllene's hoary fhade to chufe,
Or where mild Ladon's welling waters play.

I make no apology for the length of thefe quotations; the
lines of each poet are enchantingly fweet, and their beauties
were univerfally admired, till in good time Dr. Johnfon arofe
to correct the public tafte. Yet, before we extinguifh this
fplendor, cumbrous as it may be deemed, let me prefume to
fuggeft to his confideration that it is of the effence of Poetry
to give locality to perfons and things : thus Apollo is bathing
his locks in the pure dews of Caftalia, or rejoicing in his
native Delos ; the Mufes are Aonian or Pierian ; the lyre is
Lefbian or Æolian; the bow is Parthian ; the arrow Cydonian,
and the fword a rude barbarian from the mines of Scythia :
the claffic Mufe delights in this pomp of diction ; it is the
robe of ftate with which fhe arrays her felf, and let no rude
hand prefume to rend it from her.

An heavier charge is next prepared againft the Poet : " his
pofition is at laft falfe : in the time of Dante and Petrarch,
from whom he derives our firft fchool of Poetry, Italy was
over-run by *tyrant power* and *coward vice* ; nor was our ftate
much better when we firft borrowed the Italian arts." This
could not have been faid but through a total mifconception
of the Poet's hiftorical deduction, which, in few words, is
this, " When Conftantinople fubmitted to the arms of Ma-
homet the Great, Athens and all Greece were enflaved by the
conquering Turks ; this fatal event drove many of the moft
learned

learned Greeks into Italy, where they were liberally encouraged by the Popes and the illuftrious Houfe of Medici, under whofe patronage literature and the fine arts flourifhed for awhile : thus the Mufes

> Left their Parnaffus for the Latian plains ;

but finding them over-run with tyrant power and coward vice, they difdained to fix their refidence there, and fought a refuge in England : happily they found it : the long reign of Edward III. was an æra of glory; that of his unhappy fon was ftrongly marked with the high fpirit of liberty; in thofe times Chaucer lived and flourifhed, greatly favoured by both thofe kings." This juftifies the truth of Mr. Gray's pofition ; his conclufion no friend to virtue and literature will con-trovert.

The firft Englifh Poet here mentioned is Shakefpear. What the Critic fays of the mythological birth given him arifes from a miftake : Milton indeed has done this, where he calls him *Fancy's Child* ; Mr. Gray fays nothing of his birth ; he ftyles him Nature's Darling, and fays that *the* Mighty Mother un-veiled her aweful face to him when a child ; to fignify the glow of his imagination, fhe is reprefented as giving him a pencil ; whofe colours richly paint the vernal year ; and, to exprefs his power over the paffions, two golden keys, one of which unfocks the gates of joy, the other thofe of terror and pity : this is happily conceived, and expreffed with clear and elegant fimplicity. The feraphic fublimity of Milton is great-ly charafterifed. " The car of Dryden, fays the Critic, with his two courfers, has nothing in it peculiar ; it is a car

in

in which any other rider may be placed." More judgement as
well as candor had been fhown in pointing out the Pindaric
imagery, and obferving that this car is borne wide over the
fields of glory by

Two courfers of ethereal race,
With necks in thunder cloath'd, and long-refounding pace.

The mention of Dryden's Ode in honour of St. Cecilia's day
is unnoticed : the richnefs of imagination, the felicity of expreffion, and the fweetnefs of numbers, with which that noble
torrent of enthufiafm is celebrated, could not extort praife, but
they ftrike cenfure dumb. The latter part of this concluding
ftanza fhows at leaft that Mr. Gray had the uncommon
happinefs to fpeak of himfelf with grace ; but it is the province of the Critic to place him in that high ftation in the
realms of Poetry, which his own modefty would not allow him
to affume.

From the moft elegant and moft pleafing we come now to
the grandeft and fublimeft effort of the Lyric Mufe : forcible
conception, a fervor of enthufiafm, and a terrible greatnefs
characterife the Bard. They, who think it an imitation of the
Prophecy of Nereus, depreciate this Ode through a partial
fondnefs for antiquity ; it is the genuine production of Mr.
Gray's vigorous genius, animated perhaps by fome wonderful
paffages of Æfchylus. But the fuppofition ferves well enough
to introduce Dr. Johnfon's cold and taftelefs Criticifm. " To
copy, fays he, is lefs than to invent, and the copy has been
unhappily produced at a wrong time. The fiction of Horace
was to the Romans credible ; but its revival difgufts us with

apparent

apparent and unconquerable falsehood. To select a singular
event, and swell it to a giant's bulk by fabulous appendages
of spectres and predictions, has little difficulty, for he that
forsakes the probable may always find the marvellous." And
again, " in the third stanza we have the puerilities of obsolete
mythology. When we are told that *Cadwallo hush'd the stormy
main*, and that *Modred* made *huge Plinlimmon bow his cloud top'd
head*, attention recoils from the repetition of a tale that, even
when it was first heard, was heard with scorn." The mis-
fortune is, this Critic is for regulating poetic imagination by
the standard of methodical argumentation and philosophical
truth; as if the excursions of Shakespear's fancy were to be
measured by the theorems of Euclid. Fiction is the province
of this kind of poetry, which delights in the marvellous that
barely comes within the verge of possibility: it has an ideal
world of its own peopled with imaginary beings, and builds its
agreeable delusions on the light foundations of fancy, popular
belief, old traditions, and vulgar superstitions; hence, as a
fine writer observes *, " the Poet, who can give to splendid
inventions and to fictions new and bold, the air and authority
of reality and truth, is master of the genuine sources of the
Castalian spring, and may justly be said to draw his inspira-
tion from the *well-head of pure poesy.*

On these principles the antients allowed the mythological
fictions of their Poets, though in reality no more credible to
them than later superstitions are to us ; and in all ages popular belief has been the allowable foundation of poetic fiction.

---

* Essay on the Writings and Genius of Shakespear.

6

" Even

" Even when a popular opinion has long been exploded, and has become repugnant to univerfal belief, the fictions built upon it are ftill admitted as natural, becaufe (fays the * philofophical Critic) they were accounted fuch by the people to whom they were firft addreffed; whofe fentiments and views of things we are willing to adopt, when, by the power of pleafing defcription, we are introduced into their fcenes, and made acquainted with their manners." Wretched as the mythology in Offian's Poems is, attention recoils not from the delirious fancy, but we feel ourfelves impreffed with the ideas of the Northern Bard, and even catch his enthufiafm: I envy not the heart that can turn, with an incredulus odi, from images like this, " Trenmor came from his hill at the voice of his mighty Son. A cloud, like the fteed of the ftranger, fupported his aery limbs. His robe is like the mift of Lano, that brings death to the people. His fword is a green meteor half-extinguifhed. His face is without form, and dark. He fighed thrice over the Hero; and thrice the winds of the night roared around."—The war of Caros.—

On thefe principles we admit the Spirit of the Cape in the Lufiad of Camoens, the Witches and Fairies of Shakefpear, his aerial Beings attendant on Profpero, and the delicate machinery of the Sylphs in the Rape of the Lock.

> Sans tous ces ornaments le vers tombe en langueur;
> La Poefie eft morte, ou rampe fans vigueur :
> Le poëte n' eft plus qu' un orateur, timide,
> Qu' un froid hiftorien d' une fable infipide.—Boileau.

* Dr. Beattie's Effay on Poetry &c. Part i. ch. ii.

But

But this fubject, particularly as it relates to Gothic and Celtic fuperftitions and manners, has been treated with fo much precifion and elegance by the two beft Critics of this or any other age, that one is aftonifhed to find a perfon, who has read the Letters on Chivalry, and the Difcourfe on Præter-natural Beings in the Effay on the Genius and Writings of Shakefpear, fpeaking with contempt of the Magnanima Men-fogna of the Bard.

The Critic feems almoft to have contented himfelf with his general cenfure of the poetic fiction; he makes but few ob-jections to particular paffages of this Ode; and thefe are in the fame fpirit of arbitrary and unmannered Criticifm. " The Stanzas, he fays, are too long, efpecially his Epodes." Pindar has many longer. " Of the firft ftanza the abrupt beginning has been celebrated; but technical beauties can give praife only to the inventor." The rules of Art are deduced from original beauties, and all beauties will give praife to every writer, who ufes them with judgement. It is the praife of Homer that he hurries his reader in medias res non fecus ac notas: does the fame artful management devolve no praife on Virgil, becaufe the beauty is technical? Mr. Gray's Ode muft have a beginning; if he has formed it with judgement, if it is fuch as the fituation of the Bard feems to require, it has been juftly celebrated. But " it is in the power of any man to rufh abruptly upon his fubject, that has read the ballad of Johnny Armftrong,

Is there ever a man in all Scotland ——"

The

The Critic here affects to be pleasant,

afper

Incolumi gravitate jocum tentavit :

it is equally in the power of any man to rush upon a rude jest, who does not feel abashed at offending against delicacy and good manners.

" The initial resemblances, or alliterations, *ruin, ruthless, helm nor hauberk*, are below the grandeur of a poem that endeavours at sublimity." Of this figure, for with that name it has been dignified, much might be said, much has been said, and enough for every good purpose by the late excellent Mr. Harris in his Philological Inquiries. Part II. Ch. iv. Perhaps this concurrence of the letters was merely accidental ; be that as it will, the words are the moft proper for the Poet's purpose of any in our language ; and furely it would have been a ridiculous affectation in him to have gone out of his way and have chosen worse, becaufe these happened to have initial refemblances. After all, what occasion of censure do they give ? Should Dr. Johnson reprobate the second lines of these beautiful couplets,

New forrow rifes, as the day returns,
A fifter fickens, or a daughter mourns.

Vanity of Human Wishes.

Ye glitt'ring train ! whom Lace and Velvet blefs,
Sufpend the foft follicitudes of drefs.

Prologue to Irene.

Our daring Bard, with fpirit unconfin'd,
Spreads wide the mighty moral for mankind. — Ib.

no

no perfon, who has an ear, would take part with the Critic.
But thefe lines, it may be faid, affect not grandeur, endeavour
not at fublimity. Let us then turn to fuch as do, and hear
the heroic Leontius,

> And is it thus Demetrius meets his friend,
> Hid in the mean difguife of Turkifh robes,
> With fervile fecrefy to lurk in fhades——

Again,

> The groaning Greeks break up their golden caverns——

Once more,

> The dreadful diffonance of barb'rous triumph —

Nor muft we omit the Moral of this tragedy,

> Weak man with erring rage may throw the dart,
> But heav'n fhall guide it to the guilty heart.

The weaving of the winding fheet Mr. Gray borrows, as
he owns, from the Northern Bards; therefore it is not, what
this Critic's harfh language ftyles it, *Theft.* He defcribes the
flaughtered Bards as weaving the web; but was this *work of
death* only proper for women, becaufe in another mythology
the thread of life was fpun by female hands? Is the fiction out-
rageous and incongruous, which was adopted from the wild
but animated ideas of the Bards of thofe times? — Whether
the Poet has ufed the words *warp* and *woof* with propriety we
fhall be able to judge when Dictionary-makers fhall have
fettled the precife meaning of thofe terms; in the mean time
the public probably will not think itfelf deeply interefted in
the queftion.

I cannot

I cannot quit this subject without taking a review of the Ode. The Bard, as Dr. Beattie, who caught the enthusiasm of the Poet, finely observes, " just escaped from the Massacre of his brethren, under the complicated agitations of grief, revenge, and despair, and surrounded with the scenery of rocks, mountains, and torrents, stupendous by nature, and now rendered hideous by desolation, imprecates perdition upon the bloody Edward." The effect of this imprecation on the tyrant and his warrior chiefs is greatly represented by images of varied terror; the king's crested pride was dismayed;

Stout Glo'ster stood aghast in speechless trance :
To arms ! cried Mortimer, and couch'd his quiv'ring lance.

The description of the Bard adds to the great ideas of Raphael and Milton a wild dignity of sorrow which strikes us with awe. His lamentations over his slaughtered brethren call for revenge in strains of dreadful harmony. Amidst these wo-wild notes he sees their spirits sitting on a distant cliff, and weaving the ample winding-sheet of Edward's race; on this, " seized with prophetic enthusiasm, he foretells in the most alarming strains, and typifies by the most dreadful images the disasters that were to overtake his family and descendents." And now, " The work is done." The airy images melt away in a track of light that fires the western skies. Yet other visions, visions of glory, now burst upon his sight; he beholds in a a prophetic extasy a succession of genuine kings, of the line of Tudor, regain their sovereignty; the deep sorrows of his lyre are now changed to measures of transport and rapture; he hails the Bards of future times, whose voices

reach his ear, and with ftrains of defiance and triumph, fee-
ing his death inevitable, (like the poor mariner that leaps
from his burning fhip into the fea) to preferve himfelf from
the outrages of his enemies he plunges from the mountain's
height into the roaring tide below.

The wild and romantic fcenery, the ftrength of conception,
the boldnefs of the figures, the terrible fublimity, the folemn
fpirit of prophecy, and the animated glow of vifions of glory
render this " the fineft Ode in the world." The language of
Gray is always pure, peculiarly compact and nervous, ever appropriated to his fubject; when that is gay and fmiling, his
diction is elegant and glittering; in the fober reflections of
faintly melancholy it is grave and folemn; and it rifes with an
elevated dignity along with the boldeft flights of his fublime
imagination; and his numbers, regulated by a fine tafte and a
nice ear, have through all their various modulations a rich
and copious harmony. Gray inherited the ample pinion of
the Theban Eagle, and fails with fupreme dominion through
the azure deep of air; but he never finks to that humiliating
lownefs to which not want of genius, but the poverty of his
fubject often depreffes the Theban's fluttering pennons: he
therefore has a claim to the higheft rank in the realms of
Lyric Pcety. This teftimony to his merit would from any
lover of literature have been an act of juftice; but from the
tranflator of Æfchylus, who owes fo much to him, it is a debt
of Gratitude.

What could induce Dr. Johnfon, who as a good man might
be expected to favour goodnefs, as a fcholar to be candid to a
man of learning, to attack this excellent perfon and poet with
fuch

fuch outrage and indecency, we can only conjecture from this obfervation, " there muſt be a certain fympathy between the book and the reader to create a good liking." Now it is certain that the Critic has nothing of this fympathy, no portion nor fenfe of that vivida vis animi, that etherial flame which animates the poet ; he is therefore as little qualified to judge of thefe works of imagination, as the fhivering inhabitant of the caverns of the North to form an idea of the glowing fun that flames over the plains of Chili.

Dr. Johnfon knows well that " all Truth is valuable, and that fatyrical criticifm may be confidered as ufeful, when it rectifies error and improves judgement ; he that refines the publick tafte is a publick benefactor." Under this idea he will value the truth of thefe obfervations ; and upon a more careful review of this Ode of Gray he will perhaps difcover that it has fome little ufe, that it promotes one truth ; " it makes kings fear to be tyrants, tyrants to manifeſt their tyrannical humours." Few indeed are the pages any where to be found from which fome ufeful inftruction may not be derived by thofe who are difpofed to receive it ; even thefe may be a leſſon to literary tyrants to bear their faculties meekly, to favour the Progrefs of Poetry, and to fpare the Bard.

THE NINTH

PYTHIAN ODE

OF

PINDAR

TRANSLATED.

THE NINTH

PYTHIAN ODE

O F

PINDAR.

To TELESICRATES of CYRENE,

VICTOR IN THE FOOT RACE IN ARMOUR.

HIGH the willing song I raise,
 The deep-zon'd Graces aid the strain
Tun'd to the Pythian victor's praise,
His brazen shield borne o'er the plain.
Blest Youth, Cyrene's pride and grace,
Fam'd for her manag'd coursers gen'rous race.
Her once in Pelion's rustling vales,
His loose locks streaming to the wanton gales,

Apollo

Apollo feiz'd ; and thence convey'd
To Libya's paftur'd plains, and cultur'd fields,
High on his golden car the huntrefs maid ;
To the lov'd Fair thofe blooming regions yields ;
Fixes her feat in that delightful land,
A third of Earth's firm globe beneath her foft command.

ANTISTROPHE.

Silver-fandal'd Venus there
Her hand with courteous grace addreft,
And lightly touch'd the heav'n-wrought car,
Proud to receive her Delian gueft ;
Then their fweet bridal bed t'adorn
Sent Modefty foft-blufhing like the Morn ;
Thus to the god his virgin bride,
From wide-commanding Hypfeus fprung, affied.
He, from the monarch of the main
The fecond in defcent, illuftrious name,
Held o'er the haughty Lapithæ his reign :
Him in the vales of Pindus known to fame
A Naid, Nymph from Gaia fprung, of yore
Of her Penëus proud the fond Creufa bore.

EPODE.

Beneath his royal roof
The fair Cyrene's opening bloom
The monarch nurtur'd with a parent's pride.
Her nor the labours of the loom,
While through the trembling woof
The quick-returning fhuttle learns to glide,

Nor

Nor the rich pleasures of the feast
Amidst the female band, delight :
But the bright spear, the arrow wing'd for flight,
And in the chace to pierce the savage beast;
That safe through pastur'd mead and grove
Her father's herds in peace might rove :
At morn's approach she seeks a short repose;
Sleep on her couch attends her willing eyes to close.

S T R O P H E II.

Her the distant-wounding god,
His quiver rattling by his side
As down the rocky steep he trod,
With a fierce lion grappling spied ;
Alone he saw the virgin stand,
Nor spear nor falchion arm'd her daring hand :
To Chiron strait his voice addrest,
Haste, Son of Phillyra, at my request
Come from thy venerable cave ;
See and admire this virgin ; undismaid
See that fair form the dang'rous conflict brave,
A force, a spirit above the toil display'd :
Say from what root this lovely plant is sprung,
Sweet-blooming 'midst these crags with darksome shades
    o'erhung.

A N T I S T R O P H E.

Ardent see her noble fire
Amidst the fierce encounter glow.

Indulgent

Indulgent to my fond defire
My hand will Heav'n's juft Pow'r allow
To feize her, and in this bleft hour
Crop from its verdant ftalk this honied flow'r?
With afpect mild and courteous grace,
A confcious fmile bright-glowing on his face,
The gen'rous Centaur thus replied,
Perfuafion is the key of hallow'd Love;
That can unlock the fecrets this would hide;
Alike in men below, in gods above,
When firft they feel the foul-enkindling flame,
A modeft awe forbids their foft defire to name.

E P O D E.

Thee, to whom Falfehood's tongue
Dares not the guileful fable feign,
Thy gentle manners thus to fpeak incline.
Doft thou, O royal Phoebus, deign
Afk whence this virgin fprung?
The deftin'd end of all things it is thine,
And all their various ways, to know:
How many leaves in fpring are feen
Wave o'er the genial earth their chearful green;
Where the vaft ocean beats, where rivers flow,
How many fands the fhores contain
By wild winds roll'd or billowy main:
Doth not thine eye whate'er the fates decree,
Th' events of future times, and whence they fpring, forefee?

STROPHE

S T R O P H E   III.

Muſt I vie then with the wife ?
Then I will ſpeak.   The virgin bride,
The bridegroom thou, thy lovely prize,
From this rude vale art come to guide ;
Her o'er the ocean ſhalt thou bear,
And in Jove's fragrant garden place the Fair,
Collected there the iſland train,
Where the mount ſwells amidſt th' encircling plain.
In ſplendid manſions rich with gold
Libya, for wide-extended meads renown'd,
Exulting ſhall th' illuſtrious Nymph behold ;
And, that on Laws an empire ſhe may found,
Part of her realms aſſign, her queen to grace,
Not bare of fruitful plants, nor void of beaſts of chace.

A N T I S T R O P H E.

There a ſon ſhall crown thy love :
Him from the raptur'd mother's care
The noble Hermes ſhall remove,
And to the * Hours and Gaia bear,
Whoſe gorgeous feats their ſtate diſplay ;
They on their knees the ſmiling babe ſhall lay,
Shall Nectar through his lips diſtill,
And with Ambroſia, food celeſtial, fill! ;

* This is ſaid with great propriety : as the Patron of agriculture he was to
be inſtructed by the Hours quo ſidere terram vertere ; by Gaia, arvorum quæ
robora cuique.

Immortal

Immortal as his facred fire,

As Jove immortal fhall they raife the boy ;

Him fhall his friends their dear delight admire,

O'er fpatious plains to lead the flocks his joy ;

Thy Ariftæus thus fhall rife to fame,

And him the Hunter fome, and fome the Shepherd
    name.

E P O D E.

His words enchanting found

Swell the fond wifh of rapt'rous love.

Ardent the gods, difdaining cold delay,

Swift by fhort ways to action move.

That day his wifhes crown'd.

Around their couch the Loves in Libya play,

Where o'er the ftately-ftructur'd town,

High fam'd on Pytho's facred plain,

The god delighted holds his guardian reign ;

Whence Telefīcrates now brings renown,

And binds, whilft Fortune radiant glows,

Frefh wreaths around Cyrene's brows ;

Back to his country, feat to Beauty dear,

Pleas'd fhe the victor fees the prize of glory bear.

S T R O P H E IV.

Virtues greatly eminent

Swell the full pomp of copious praife :

But he, the noble argument

Who brief in fplendid phrafe difplays,

Delights

(47)

Delights the wife: whate'er you trace,

* Occasion gives it energy and grace.

Thebes, for seven towred gates renown'd,

Saw Iolaus of old with glory crown'd;

And when avenging barb'rous pride,

His falchion thunder'd on the tyrant's head,

Car-borne Amphitryon's honour'd tomb beside

Laid in her hallow'd earth the hero dead

His grandfire nigh: Thebes once the stranger's car

Saw 'midst her dragon race his snowy coursers bear.

---

* The conduct of the Poet in this Ode deserves our attention. He begins by declaring his desire to celebrate the victory of Telesicrates in the Pythian Games; but conscious of the barrenness of his subject,

> Exigua cum frænaret materia impetum,

after five lines he leaves his hero to record the history of the Nymph Cyrene, nor does he return to him till towards the middle of the third Epode, and in six lines more his praise is again interrupted. Though a reader of taste, not interested in the encomium, may not only forgive him, but be highly pleased with the very beautiful digression, yet he might well fear that Telesicrates would receive it otherwise, and, like the Pycta to Simonides, bid him go to his Cyrene for his reward. This accounts for the reflection in the beginning of this Strophe, which is an artful and delicate apology for his own conduct in the preceding part of the Ode, where so much is given to Cyrene, and so little to Telesicrates: he then shows that the seasonable introduction of a circumstance is the crown of all praise, by an allusion to the story of Iolaus: nor is this hero introduced at random; for, besides his near connexion with Hercules and his sons, whose descendents were among the first colonists at Cyrene, the circumstance of his being buried near the tomb of Amphitryon leads him naturally to the mention of Hercules and Iphicles, the institutors of the Games in which Telesicrates had been Conqueror: this brings him back to his first proposed design, Πυθιονικᾶν Τελεσικράτη γεγωνῖν, which he then does amply, and with uncommon spirit: thus are his bold transitions well connected and coherent.

ANTISTROPHE.

ANTISTROPHE.

Sprung from his and Jove's embrace
Two fons, together giv'n to light,
To high thoughts rais'd Alcmena grace,
Sons of immenfe, unconquer'd might.
Dumb is the tongue untaught to found
Thy name, Alcides, through the world renown'd;
That fings not Dirce's ftreams, which roll'd
To nurture thee and Iphicles of old:
Grateful your praife will I difplay,
Your bounties hymning high in founding ftrain:
Mine ever be the Graces' brighteft ray.
The mount of Nifus, and Ægina's plain
Saw thee thrice victor raife Cyrene's name,
Nor dark Defpair was thine, nor filent-grieving Shame.

EPODE.

Cyrene's fons among
Doth one with gen'rous friendfhip glow?
Is there whofe dark'ning bofom fwells with hate?
Free let them give his praife to flow,
Roll the full tide along,
And hail the labours glorious to the ftate:
Praife e'en a foe who feeks renown
By juft and gen'rous deeds to gain;
So taught the hoary prophet of the main.
Thine, Teleficrates, th' Olympic crown;
Thee victor oft Minerva's feaft,
Thy country oft with pride addreft;

Her

Her fon each mother wifh'd thee, and with fighs
Silent each virgin felt Love's foftest wifh arife.

STROPHE V.

Me, though eager my defire
Th' impetuous courfe of Song to rein,
Hark! hear you not a voice require
Once more to roll the grateful strain,
Great deeds once more with fame to grace,
And raife the antient glory of thy race?
Iraffa (there in royal ftate
High on his honour'd throne Antæus fate)
The fuitor train attending faw;
Ardent to win the Libyan Fair they vied,
Princes, their blood from the fame fource who draw,
And foreign Chiefs demand the beauteous bride;
For her bright hair in golden ringlets flows,
And on her blufhing cheek Love's brightest lustre glows.

ANTISTROPHE.

Whilst each raptur'd Wooer fought
This gold-crown'd flow'r of youth to gain,
The monarch ftrove with anxious thought
The noblest nuptials to obtain:
He heard how Danaus of old,
E'er half its courfe the radiant day had roll'd,
In fhortest fpace at Argos found
With bridal wreaths his fifty daughters crown'd:
Rang'd at the goal the virgin band,
A radiant line, the father will'd to place;

Then

Then to th' impatient lovers gave command
To wing with flying feet the rapid race;
Thus sage decreed all contests to decide,
And, as they reach'd the goal, each hero chose his bride.

E P O D E.

The Libyan thus decreed
To highest worth the royal maid :
Her a bright mark the lengthen'd course to bound,
In radiant-tinctur'd robes array'd,
He plac'd, the victor's meed ;
And thus addrefs'd the youths that clos'd him round ;
Let him, who first shall touch her vest,
Lead her, his toils to crown, his prize.
Swift as the wind Alexidamus flies,
And with his hand her hand enraptur'd preft ;
Then led her to his warlike train,
Whose proud steeds paw'd Numidia's plain ;
They scatter'd round him wreaths and verdant boughs,
As Conquest oft before with laurels bound his brows.

www.ingramcontent.com/pod-product-compliance
Lightning Source LLC
Chambersburg PA
CBHW021643270326
41931CB00008B/1138